"THE PANDORA'S BOX"

The forbidden truth about dating and relationships

By:
Alessio David Ricioppo Parra

Hey, my name is
Alessio David Ricioppo Parra.
Life and dating coach!
I help people achieving
their maximum potential!

About the author:

Alessio David Ricioppo Parra (born in Genoa on 21st september 1988, with double spanish and italian citizenship) is a life and dating coach and an advanced yogi who started to practice yoga at the age of 16 and that loves to help people to be happier, to grow in a better version of themself and achieving their dreams.

copyright ©
Year of release - 2017
Alessio David Ricioppo Parra
THE PANDORA'S BOX
The forbidden truth about dating and relationships.

ISBN 978-0-244-93453-8
Published thanks to: lulu.com
All rights reserved

Official website: theinteriorlight.wordpress.com
Official business mail (feedback, life and dating coaching requests): theinteriorlight@gmail.com

INTRODUCTION AND ACKNOWLEDGEMENTS

This book was requested by clients as a follow up of my book *"The Interior Light – Activate your greatness"* (available on <u>lulu.com</u>) as a more detailed analysis of dating and relationships. When you will read this book, the truth about dating and relationships will be fully opened to you. And once it's opened, you will not be able to unsee it. This is the *"forbidden truth"* that feminists and society don't want people to know and they try to hide at all costs. Dear reader, you might ask me: *"Why the choice of this title?"*. In Greek mythology the Pandora's box was a box in which they were sealed all the evils of the world, however Pandora was so curious about it that she eventually decided to open the box, causing all the evils to escape from the box and leaving only *"hope"* in the bottom of the opened box. Today you are also faced with the possibility to open a box. But this time, when the box is open, it will be all the evil illusions and lies that feminists and society tried and try to implant in everyone about dating and relationship that will be gone, leaving available at the end of the box only the truth behind dating and relationships. This truth will be yours for your whole life, thus improving and allowing you to have effortless dating and relationship skills... That's why I decided to call this book *"The Pandora's box"*.
I strongly recommend you to read this book at least 10-15 times and practice to the point that the principles of this book become fully instinctive for you and you will become an alpha of your respective gender (alpha man, alpha woman). This book is especially dedicated to all my clients and to the people who made it possible. You know who you are and thanks to all of you! Are you ready to open the box?...
Yeah of course you are, let's go!!! =-)
Good reading!

Coach Ricioppo Parra

SUMMARY

THE SPARK OF ATTRACTION

"He is so different from the others" - Yana taught as soon as she looked in his eyes... This happened during a white night in Saint Petersburg.

Yana is a brilliant and stunning model: brown and long hair, blue eyes and a great shape.

She was passing a very harsh period as she had a bad breakup with her ex boyfriend Igor a few weeks before that night.

Their relationship had been going for long and having invested so much time and energy in this relationship, Yana felt completely devastated at the end of the relationship to the point that for several weeks she didn't want to go out, forcing herself to pretty much do just her work.

Essenia was very worried about her. Essenia is Yana's best friend and also a model: blonde and long hair, brown eyes and a great shape as well. They know each other since many years, but this was the first time that Essenia saw Yana in such a bad mood and pitiful state.

Essenia was able to make Yana talk about what happened, but no matter what Yana still refused to go out outside working.

Essenia respected that but as several weeks passed by after the break up, she couldn't just stay there and watch. Essenia called Yana that afternoon: *"Yana! I know that you feel bad, but if you continue to stay the whole time thinking about this, you might depress. I have an idea, what about we go out to a funny party? It will keep you busy for a while so you will not think about that matter".*

Yana appreciated the call and told Essenia: *"You are right Essenia. I need to keep myself busy and think about something else. Let's go to this party, but remember that tomorrow we have a lot of work to do together, starting early in the morning. Around midnight we ought to get out of the party and return home."*. Essenia replied: *"Of course sweetheart, I'll pick up you at 20:00 in front of your house. See you later, kisses"*. Essenia went to pick up Yana, she complimented Yana for her dress then they went to the party. The party was organized by a friend of Essenia, Anastasia. As they arrived, Anastasia warmly welcomed Essenia and Essenia introduced her to Yana. *"Feel yourself like home, if you need something just ask. Have fun!"* - Anastasia said to Yana and Essenia and then she returned to her errands. The club that Anastasia rented for the party was big, with cool music in the background and a lot of people – both men and women. That night a lot of dudes tried to approach Yana.

Most of them were totally clueless, using some used pick up lines like *"You are a thief, because you stole my heart"*, *"You look a lot like Irina Shayk"*, *"Can I buy you a drink?"*, *"I was wondering if we could go out sometimes"* and several other weak approaches on those lines.

Neither of them really stand out: the first approach almost made her puke, the second didn't made her feel special and unique, the third dude was trying to foolishly seek her approval and the fourth was apparently just completely lacking any kind of confidence. Since some of them were pretty insistent, she asked for their business cards instead of giving them her number to make them go away (throwing the business card away not long after when they weren't looking at her).

Some approaches instead were decent and she gave away her number.

Time was almost up, it was almost midnight. Yana and Essenia were preparing to go away, when their eyes noticed something unusual.

In the depths of the club there were two men having a lot of fun and they weren't there approaching women like all the other dudes there.

They were so laid back, having a lot of fun talking to each other, listening to music and laughing.

Yana and Essenia noticed as several women passed there, talked a few minutes having a fun talk with them and then proceeding in another direction of the club. *"Who are they?"* - Yana and her friend said to each other. That's when Yana looked in the eyes of one of them. His presence was completely different from the other dudes that tried to hit on her that night. Yana smiled at him and she was a bit nervous as he waved playfully a finger as a signal to invite her to come to him. Yana was looking at him shocked thinking *"What? Why doesn't he approach me first like all the other dudes here?!"* and tried to wave a finger to invite him to come to her instead.

In response he said no with his head and insisted by waving his finger inviting her again to come in and at that point she couldn't contain herself anymore from the curiosity. *"I'll check in by myself, but you can join if you want"* said Yana to Essenia.

Yana went to them and asked *"Hey! What's up? Do you enjoy the party?"* while in particular looking in the eyes of the man who invited her to come in.

He started to talk *"Yeah, we're having a lot of fun."* as the man get a bit closer to her and said to her by looking in her eyes *"You are amazing, you take my breath away. You're intoxicating to look at. What's your name?"*. Yana was positively surprised by how direct and confident this man was. She replied to him *"I'm Yana, it's nice to meet you. What's your name?"*. The man replied to her: *"Nice to meet you too! My name is Diego and this is my friend Emilio. We are close friends of the organizer of the party"*. **(When a woman is interested and a man asks her name without offering his, the woman will ask back his name.).**

As Diego said that, Essenia also arrived to see what was happening and introduced herself to the two of them. Diego and his friend started to joke a bit with them and they noticed that Essenia stated that unfortunately it was midnight and they had to go. Diego noticed it and said: *"Wait a moment, are we in a Cinderella show?"* and as Yana started to laugh, he said: *"Essenia, I will borrow your friend Yana just for a minute before you two go"*.

Diego took Yana apart from her friend and said firmly to her by looking at her eyes: *"I want you Yana.*

I know that now you need to go away with your friend, so what's your number?" as he pulled out his phone. Yana was surprised by such directness so she gave him the number without any hesitation and he gave her his as well. At that point Yana and Diego returned to the table and Diego said to Essenia *"Cinderella is ready now! I wish you a great night, girls!"*. Yana and Essenia laughed, said good night too and then proceeded to return home. Essenia told to her that she also got the number from Emilio, that offered her directly his number and saying to contact him if she had some cool plans in mind and she gave him hers. Yana and Essenia started to comment on how different Diego and Emilio were compared to the other dudes of the club. Very direct and confident, straight to the point and fun to be around. Yana commented on how Diego's presence was dominating, yet playful and kind at the same time. It was something refreshing that she didn't see in a long time. Yana thanked Essenia for the invite and the funny evening, then they returned home. It was clear that the spark of attraction happened between Yana and Diego that night *(For a man in order to have a shot with a woman, she needs to have at least a minimal level of attraction in which case it's possible to increase it, otherwise move on. It's important to gauge the attraction of the woman as soon as engaging in a conversation. The more a woman likes a man, the more she helps him and the easier is to get her contact information. Confident and highly interested women will approach men first and even straight ask him to go out together).*

<u>THE DAY AFTER</u>

Yana wakes up early and calls Essenia: *"Essenia, thanks for yesterday! It was funny. We have that photosession together, Maksim waits us in his study at 11:00".* Essenia: *"You're welcome, yeah I remember. See you later there!".*

Maksim is one of the professional photographers with whom Yana and Essenia sometimes works for their portfolios. After the photosession they agree on all the needed last details about the new portfolio, after this Maksim confirms that he will call them as soon as ready for retiring it. After that Yana and Essenia go to have lunch together and they start to talk about the previous day.

Yana: *"Essenia, it was an interesting party yesterday! Have you heard Emilio?".*

Essenia: *"Not yet, what about the guys which tried to hit on you yesterday? And Diego?".*

Yana: *"When I opened the phone this morning, I noticed that some of them texted me soon after we left. Some of them tried to call me this morning before I came to work, including some that wanted just to talk instead of planning a date. Of course I didn't agree on a date with them, they were so much needy and desperate! About Diego, I haven't heard him: he hasn't called or texted yet. I wonder why...".*

Essenia: *"I see! Maybe is Diego simply busy at the moment?".*

Yana: *"It could be indeed the case, but I am still wondering a lot about him. He seems so different from the others...".*

Essenia: *"Yes and his friend Emilio too. I wonder when we are going to hear from them".*

As Essenia just said that, Yana's phone starts to ring. Essenia: *"Is that Diego?".*

Yana looked at the phone: *"...No, he is not Diego. He is my best male friend Fjodar. Wait a minute".*

Fjodar: *"Hi Yana!".*

Yana: *"Hey Fjodar! What's up?".*

Fjodar: *"Great. Remember that favour you asked me? I found that book which you asked about. Are you free this afternoon?".*

Yana: *"Great! Sure!".*

Fjodar: *"Good, see you at 5 p.m. at this bar on Nevskji Prospekt?" (he send to her a photo of it).*

Yana: *"I know that place. Ok, see you there later".*

Essenia smiles and says: *"Do you have a romantic date with him?".*

Yana smiles and says: *"You know that I consider him only a friend. I asked him a favour time ago and he managed to find a book I have been searching".*

Essenia: *"What is this book about?".*

Yana: *"I will show you better directly in person. It looks very interesting".*

Essenia: *"Sure, no problem!".*

Yana and Essenia finished lunching, then they went to the commercial center to buy something. Afterwards they greeted each other as Yana was going to see Fjodar.

Fjodar and Yana greet each other with an hug.
Fjodar - *"It's so nice to meet you dear Yana"*.
Yana - *"Mutually, Fjodar!"*.

They order a take away coffee as Fjodar pays and
then they sit on a nearby green area. They start to
talk for several minutes about the recent things that
happened in their life, then Fjodar takes the book out
of his pocket.

*"Yana, this is the book that you wanted. It arrived
yesterday in my house by post so I bringed it for you
as soon as possible! No need to pay me, it's a
gift."* said Fjodar to Yana.

"Thank you very much! I appreciate" replies Yana as
she puts the book away. Then Fjodar voice starts to
have a much serious tone.

*"Yana, I need to talk with you about a certain
matter."* says Fjodar.

"About what?" replies with curiosity Yana.

*"Yana... I wanted to say you this much earlier but..
you see... I love you... Do you want to be my
girlfriend?"* says Fjodar to Yana.

A prolonged and awkward moment of silence
starts as Yana is thinking about how he tried to bribe
her affection with a gift and how inappropriate such
a request was. **(Women tend to fall in love slowly, it
takes usually around 7/8+ weeks of dating to open up
their heart and bring up labels the exclusivity talk.)**

"Fjodar, I am not interested in you, I'm very sorry"
Fjodar starts to act unglued and argue with her:
"What? What do you mean? I even bought a gift!"

Yana starts to feel more awkward and replies:
"Fjodar, I really appreciate the gift, but I don't want to go out with you romantically".

Fjodar: *"Why don't you want to go out with me?. After all I did for you? I love you Yana"*.

Yana:*"I'm sorry Fjodar, but I consider you only a friend"*.

(As women tend to be driven by emotions, Yana used a circle of words because she didn't want to hurt Fjodar, hoping that Fjodar got the hint and left her alone. But Fjodar worsened the situation by acting unglued and starting to argue logically with her. Rule number one: never argue with a woman. Women want either to be opened up emotionally or to be put in their place if they behave disrespectfully in order to feel the masculine strength of the man.)

Soon after hearing that, Fjodar says to her: *"I see, good evening and all the best",* Yana wishes the best for him too and Fjodar goes away with a broken look in his eyes.

(The best way to turn a friend in a romantic partner is to gauge if there is at least a minimal level of attraction to work with. The quickest and safest way to do this is to make obvious that you like the friend and observe the reaction. If nothing happens then you completely back off and just answer to the friend's call, text or sms when the friend reaches out to you, letting the friend do 100% effort and reciprocating the same amount of effort the friend does. Now, if the friend has at least the minimal needed amount of romantic interest, the friend will sense your complete back off and bring up the topic of you being colder and more distant. In that case, it means that the friend has romantic interest

in you and you can invite the friend to meet up romantically in a date: from that point on, the interaction will be treated as a courtship and follow the flow of sexual polarity.

Otherwise if the friend doesn't bring the topic of your complete back off, then the friend doesn't truly care about you in a romantic sense so it's usually not advisable in this case to bring the topic of dating).

As Yana is returning home, she passes close to the restaurant in where she had the first date with Igor. A lot of memories returns to her mind about that evening date as she is returning home. As she opens the door,   Yana's cat Pallino comes to greet her. Pallino is a white cat with some gray spots and green eyes. Yana gives Pallino his dinner and then cooked something for herself.

THE CALL

Few days passed since the meeting with Fjodar.
Yana and Essenia were hanging out together.
Yana was thinking about Diego that hadn't called or
written yet, such a mysterious man.
Yana: *"You know Essenia, Diego hasn't called yet."*
Essenia: *"I see, Emilio hasn't called yet either."*
Yana: *"Diego.. He seems so different from the
others. I wonder what he is doing right now."*
**(It's scientifically proved that women are more
attracted to men whose feelings are unclear. It's the
first of the 4 horsemen of chasing, the 4 factors that
cause a woman's attraction to rise to high level and
start to chase the man).**

While having this conversation, in another part of
Piter, in the center of the city, Diego is working.

Diego is a spanish entrepreneur who lives in Russia
since several years, his business is going great and now
he is successfully closing a negotiation.

Diego: *"Great, glad to see we reached an
agreement about this deal. I wish you an amazing day
and talk to you later."* Soon after having unlocked the
negotiation, Diego picks up the phone and starts to
make a call.

In the meanwhile, Yana and Essenia are talking. In
that moment, Yana's phone starts to ring.

Essenia: *"Who is calling?"*.
Yana smiling: *"Diego!!! I will answer now!"*.
Yana: *"Hello!!!"*.
Diego: *"Hey, it's Diego! What's up?"*.

Yana: *"I was wondering when you were going to call! I'm great, thanks. You?"*.

(The vast majority of men call a woman right after getting her number or the day after. That's extremely anti-climatic and screams neediness at its finest. By waiting a few days to contact a woman after getting her number - around 4/5+ days - that man will immediately positively differentiate himself from the vast majority of men. Assuming that the woman has enough attraction to begin with, thanks to his mysterious attitude the woman will have emotional rollercoasters – the second of the 4 horsemen of chasing. This will usually increase the woman attraction even more so this man will be the one getting the date.)

Diego: *"Great thanks! It's great to hear you, I would love to see you. When are you free to meet up?"*.

Yana: *"In the next days I have a lot of work to do but I'm free during the week-end"*.

Diego: *"Great, what about we meet Saturday in front of Saint Isaac's Cathedral at 19:30?"*.

Yana: *"Ok! Where are we going?"*.

Diego: *"That's a surprise. You will see directly Saturday.."*

Yana smiling: *"That sounds interesting! See you Saturday"*.

Diego: *"Great, looking forward to seeing you Saturday, I wish you an amazing day!"*.

Yana looks at Essenia: *"Yeah, I have a date with Diego this Saturday."*.

Essenia: *"That's great!"*.
Yana: *"Let's celebrate this by doing some shopping"*
Essenia: *"Great idea. I will help you to find something amazing for the date!"*.
(When a woman is excited about a date, she will usually tell about it to her girl friends. Her closest girl friends will also help her to look prettier. The more a woman likes a man, the more she helps the man and the more fun and effortless will be the date between them.).
While shopping, Essenia's telephone rings too.
Essenia looking at Yana: *"It's Emilio"*.
Essenia: *"Hello"*.
Emilio*: "Hello, it's Emilio talking. How are you?"*
Essenia: *"Fine thanks, you?"*.
Emilio*: "Great! I would like to see you, when are you free to meet up?"*.
Essenia: *"Next week"*.
Emilio: *"Ok, what about we meet next Monday at the metro 2 exit of Gostiny Dvor at 20:00?"*.
Essenia: *"Maybe. To be sure call me back to confirm Monday morning"*.
(When a woman is not enthusiastic about hearing a man after 4-5 days after giving you her number, that tells right on the spot that her level of attraction towards him was not that high to begin with. In this case a woman might create more barriers to meet up, making more difficult for the man to set a definite date. In particular in the case of low attraction, a woman uses two tests.
The maybe date basically means *"no, but if something better doesn't come up in the meantime then why not..."*. **The other is** *"call back to confirm"*

which is similar to the "*maybe test*", but more related in this case to feel the strength of the man and see his reaction.)

Emilio: *"I have a very busy schedule Essenia. I don't do "maybe" dates or "call back to confirm". If you can't confirm for Monday, then what about we do another time?"*.

Essenia: *"Ok, we will do another time. I have to check my schedule."*.

Emilio: *"Ok, contact me when you figure out your schedule and you know when are you available for a definite date."*.

Essenia: *"Ok, have a good evening"*.

Emilio: *"Thanks, you too"*.

(When a man calls a woman and she doesn't confirm plans for the definite date by stating "*maybe*" or "*call back to confirm*", the man should never agree on going out with her based on these premises. These are signs of low attraction and there is an high chance that the woman will cancel the date at the last moment. The other person should be grateful and enthusiastic about going out with you in a date – these dates are much more fun and effortless. So in case of the woman stating "*maybe*" or "*call back to confirm*" , the man should simply withdraw the offer by stating something on the line: *"I don't do call back to confirm, I have a busy schedule. If you don't feel comfortable, what about we do another time?"* and see her reaction. If she confirms the plans then it was just a test, otherwise the man shouldn't agree to go to the date.).

THE FIRST DATE

Yana wakes up as Pallino licks her face, her cat is apparently hungry so she prepares the food for him. As she is doing this, she is thinking about today's evening... It's the day of the first date with Diego.

(A date is a fun-filled romantic opportunity for sex to happen. The man focuses more on the logistical details and flow of the date, letting the woman to relax in her femininity and letting her doing 70/80% of the talking by asking her fun questions. The main focus by the man's part is on hanging around, have fun and hook up with the woman as she gradually opens to him. The average women will usually sleep with a man after 2/3 dates. Therefore it's important to plan the dates with the mindset of treating the other person as a lover, preferably doing evening dates. It's usually better to avoid at the beginning movie dates, lunch dates, group dates and going in environments that are lousy and with low light until she is officially in love with the man. As you go in a date, you want to communicate and know the other person better... Relationships are a natural consequences of hanging around, have fun and hook up over the course of several weeks. A woman will usually bring up about being in love, labels and the topic of exclusivity by week 7+ as long as the man does everything correctly.)

Some hours passed by, and it is now afternoon. Yana sends to Essenia a picture for the dress to use in the evening. *"What do you think about it, Essenia?"*.

Essenia replies to her message: *"That's an*

amazing red dress, Yana! I'm sure that Diego will like it".

Yana: *"Yeah, I'm wondering what kind of plans he has in store. Diego is very mysterious. Let's see what happens".* **(Women usually go in dates with an attitude of "*let's just see what happens*".)**

Essenia: *"Good luck! Talk to you later!".*

It is almost time for the date: Yana prepares herself and goes to the agreed place. Diego greets her and compliments her for the dress: *"I'm glad to see you! You look amazing Yana".*

(In the dating phase, *"Less is more"*. It's better to don't exaggerate with compliments in this phase: the woman will interpret them as a bribe for sex rather that a genuine expression of appreciation. This also applies to gifts. It's usually better to reserve gifts for when the woman is totally in love and/or together in an exclusive relationship).

Yana: *"Likewise. Thanks! You too. What do you want to do?".*

Diego: *"I have already planned where to go... The place is just right there. Let's go right now.".*

(Every person has both masculine and feminine energy. In man the predominant energy is the masculine which is associated with logic, breaking barriers and purpose, while in the woman it is the feminine associated with emotion, connection and nurturing. The flow of attraction is regulated by the law of sexual polarity, in which one partner acts more masculine and the other more feminine – which is usually achieved by a masculine man paired with a feminine woman. When a woman asks a man *"What do you want to do?"* she is actually checking if the man

behaves like a leader. If the man starts to ask back to her what to do, she will ask back to him what to do as a wake-up call on the lines of *"Come on dude, will you make a decision?! You're the man and as such you are supposed to be the leader!"*. The best way to be around a woman is to act 90% in a charming James Bond style and the remaining 10% by treating her like a little bratty sister by teasing her in a playful way. Love is supposed to be playful and fun.)

Diego and Yana reached a building close to the square. Diego says: *"I made a reservation for us. It's a great place... It is an italian restaurant close to here."* as Diego opens the entrance door to let Yana in.

Yana: *"I love italian cuisine. Great idea".*

They sit at the table, see the menu and order. As they wait, Diego starts to ask her personal questions.

Diego: *"Yana, what do you like to do for fun?".*
Yana: *"I love cooking, listening music, dancing and cats. From time to time I like to read some good books. I have a cat whose name is Pallino. He is very sweet and handsome. He has a wild personality and loves to roam around. I will show you a photo right now".*

Yana shows to him a picture of her cat.

Yana: *"What about you?".*

Diego: *"I like martial arts, psychology and reading. I also like cats. I am going to show a picture of my cat. His name is Martin".*

Diego shows to her a picture of Martin. *"He loves to play with Leo. Leo is the cat of my neighbours and usually pays visit to Martin every day at the same hour, at which they go to roam around."*.

Diego shows to her a picture of Martin and Leo together.

Yana: *"How cute! That's interesting!"*.

(The one asking questions is the one in charge of the conversation. The 3 main rules in a conversation are: 1) first of all people like to talk about themselves and everything related to them; 2) find commonalities to build rapport; 3) before adding a new layer to the conversation, add value to the conversation, then proceed with a new questions. The man should let her do 70-80% of the talking by asking fun questions. The man should listen carefully: he will be tested to check if he was listening properly – passing the test if he remembers what she said. As women tend to be driven by emotions, any emotion she feels during the date it is going to be associated to the presence of the man, hence why it is important to keep the topic and conversation fun and avoid heavy topics as much as possible. Speaking of which, it's good etiquette to don't talk about exes in a date: *"Gentlemen never kiss and tell"* and women should be appreciative about the fact that you keep privacy about such topics. If you choose to violate this principle and you tell the other about an ex, keep in mind that the other person will listen to you in a such a way as wondering how you would talk about him/her if he/she will ever become your ex in the future so talk positively about the topic.)

The waitress brings the drinks: *"Here are the drinks."* and as they thank her, the waitress goes to another table. Yana suddenly asks him: *"What do you think about that woman over there?"*.

Diego smiles and replies to Yana: *"Which other girl?"* while keeping his eyes on Yana.

Yana: *"The girl over there, other side of the restaraunt"*.

Diego's eyes are all on Yana: *"I don't see which other girl you are talking about. My focus is entirely on you, Yana"*.

Yana giggled happily while playing with her hair. **(This was a test to check where the focus of the man was. During a date, a man should never start to look around other women, as this projects a vibe of *"just looking to get laid"*. The man focus should be in the woman and her body language signals. Women's signals of attraction include playing with her hair, signs of submissive body language, looking down when the man looks in her eyes etc..)**

As the evening goes on, while they drink and eat, Diego is letting her do most of the talking, giving playful answers and remaining mysterious when Yana asks back. **(Women love to fish for information and work up to know better and get the man.)**

Suddendly she asked Diego which kind of tea he likes more: *"I like more green tea. It's healthier and tastier. What about you, Yana?"*.

Yana: *"I like more black tea. To me it is better than green tea"*.

Diego: *"To each his own"*.

(Women will purposefully ask an opinion to the man and see if they can change his opinion. If he does change his opinion to match hers, it means that the man is seeking her approval and shows to her that he has no backbone: in this case, the woman will lose

respect towards him and look for another man. Approval seeking is a feminine trait, not masculine. If the man stands up for himself like we can see in the situation above, he passes the test. A woman will always test the man when she feels attraction, either subconsciously and/or consciously, to test if the man is fully centered in his masculinity).

While Diego and Yana are talking, in a closer table, other two persons choosed the restaurant as the place for their date and by looking at them it is obvious that the woman is a gold digger. She starts to ask all the kind of materialistic questions like where he lives, how much it is his salary, which kind of car he drives etc... Gold diggers are not interested in the other person, they are just interested in his/her money. An authentic person who is truly genuinely interested will not value the other person in materialistic term like house, cars, money but rather on what the other person brings in his/her life from an emotional standpoint.

Gold diggers can be both women (more often) or men: they are not good candidates for authentic and loving frequentations and relationships.

(If a person starts to ask immediately a lot of materialistic questions and/or asking expensive gifts from the get go, it's a massive red flag towards gold digging behaviours. In this case, the best approach is to avoid replying to the materialistic questions by using jokes while keeping a playful tone and if the gold digger asks gifts, then say things on the lines of *"Don't complicate things. I'm not buying you that expensive gift. Let's just hang around, have fun and see what happens."*. If the red flags continue then you should seriously consider to run like hell and never look back before getting emotionally attached, because if you get emotionally attached at that point it will become much more difficult to walk away from the gold digger. Bottom line - it depends on your intentions. Gold diggers are superficial people and can be potentially good candidates for *"fuck buddies"/"friends with benefits"/"open relationships"* as long as you are comfortable with their transaction type of mentality. But gold diggers aren't good candidates for an authentic frequentation and loving relationship, as basically their *"affection"* is not love and genuine caring about the other person, but rather the gold digger views love as a form of transaction in exchange of money and gifts. So as soon as things complicate and/or if there is a financial crisis, instead of working through it together as a couple, the gold digger will run immediately away towards a new *"money provider partner"* like nothing happened between the two of you. Remember that the best gift you can give to someone is the gift of your presence! Therefore if you are looking for a genuine and authentic frequentation, evaluate carefully the other person based on his/her actions, running like hell and never looking back as soon as you spot the trait of gold digging in the potential partner).

Returning to Yana and Diego, it is instead clear that Yana is genuinely interested in him. She didn't go in materialistic question from the get go and they are having a lot of fun in the conversation. They smile a lot and clearly enjoy each other company. Yana eventually starts to touch Diego's hand first.

Diego replicates by touching Yana too as long as she keeps the touch up, waiting for the next invitation to touch her again.

(Touching a woman is okay when she issues a conscious or subconscious invitation of touch to the man, like bumping or initiating touch herself and should be kept as long as she keeps it. The man should restart touch only when she brings the next invitation to touch her again. It's a subtle test to see if he pursues her more than she does towards him. If he acts impatient and pursues her more than she does towards him, then her attraction will slowly drop. It's always better if the woman thinks that she wants the man at least a bit more than the man wants her, otherwise her attraction will slowly drop.)

As they finish dinner, Diego: *"I offer"* and he calls the waitress asking for the bill. Looking at Yana, it's obvious that she wanted to keep talking more. The bill arrives, Diego pays and tips the waitress.

(This is a good test to check if the woman is enthusiastic about the date or not. When the man asks for the bill and she looks like she wants to talk more – it's a great signal. If she looks bored, then she didn't enjoy it much. It's usually a good etiquette for the man to offer in the first date. Always treat the staff of the places in which you go well, if a person is kind towards whom dates but then he/she starts to act unkind towards staff/waitresses/etc... it's a red flag.

The man should never take out a woman to an extravagant expensive first date – she might become spoiled plus she is not yet his girlfriend or in love. After the first date, talking about offering to the other person...

..This depends a lot on the culture of the country but it is important to keep in mind that on long term, there should be a mutual effort).

Diego opens the door for Yana, and as they exit to the street, Yana couldn't hold back anymore. She grabs Diego and kisses him.

(Women with higher attraction will make everything easier and even kiss first if they have a direct personality. Usually it's the man who should do the first move when she is receptive and open to it.

A great way to determine when the woman is ready for the first kiss is when the woman starts touching and get close and it can be especially noticed one of the two following situations: 1) Looking first at her eyes, then her lips and then again her eyes in the period of several seconds (around 7+ seconds). If she looks back at the man's lips, she is thinking about kissing the man and she is ready to be kissed - so the man should proceed to kiss her. 2) She looks at then man's lips – as soon as she does that, she will look down (use of emotional channel) then she will look somewhere else to avoid this being noticed and restart the *"triangulation"*. In this case, the man can say something along the lines of: *"It's okay"*. She will ask what is okay, and the man: *"I want to kiss you too. Now come here and bring here those beautiful lips..."*

There is also another great way. When the woman ask *"Do you have a girlfriend?"* is a signal of high interest. When she does that, the man can playfully reply: *"There is always room for one more. Why do you ask that, are you candidating for the position? I have a requirement for that."* and follow up with *" You must be a good kisser. Are you a good kisser? Prove it"*.
If she likes the man and she is not a *"structured*

woman" with a lot of self-imposed rules, she will kiss the man. Speaking about kisses, it's usually better to go for the kiss test in the first date as soon as the signals are there or at the end of the date. In any case, it's important to don't delay a physical move too much because if in 3+ dates there is still no physical contact, usually *"not structured woman"* will assume that the man is not interested and/or lacking confidence – and in this case either the man will be friendzoned or blown off.)

Diego tries to escalate, but notices that Yana is not fully ready for making out more heavily. Therefore Diego smiles and leades Yana to make sure that she gets safely to the closest metro to return home. Diego: "*I had a lot of fun, Yana. It was a great evening*".

Yana: "*Likewise Diego, it was amazing*".

They kissed again and they said *"goodnight"* to each other.

(At the end of the date even if everything was great, it's usually better not to talk about when it will be the next date, unless it's long distance and you have a limited time to see with each other in which case it's totally ok to plan the next date on the spot. In normal cases don't plan the next date at end of the current as it kills mystery. For the same reason, it's better to avoid texting the woman immediately after telling her again how awesome the date was. The average woman will sleep with a man after 2-3 dates. To accelerate the process, the man can plan the date to flow in 2-3 different places, so that every place feels to her like an extra date and asssuring that in the last one the man can do a physical move and gauge if it's appropriate to invite her somewhere more private, or she is not ready yet and thus to wait for another occasion.)

THE SECOND DATE

The day after the date, Essenia calls and asks to Yana how the date went.

Yana replies: *"It was a great date. Diego is a true gentleman".*

Essenia: *"I am glad for you!".*

Yana: *"What about we meet up this evening? I will show you the book that Fjodar ordered for me time ago. I started to read it, it is interesting!".*

Essenia: *"With pleasure. You will tell me about the date better in person. When and where?".*

Yana: *"What about at my house at 19?".*

Essenia: *"Ok, see you later".*

Soon after the call, several messages arrived on her phone, one after the other.

Yana: *"Who is writing to me so much?"*

Yana opens the screen of the phone and countless message are sent from the same person: Fjodar.

Yana: *"What does Fjodar want right now? Let's see what he wrote...".* As she opens the message, she notices that Fjodar was basically saying that he misses her a lot and begging her to be his girlfriend. Yana was not pleased at the message, especially after having been clear in person about the matter.

(Begging is a weak negotiating position that shows disrespect. And without respect there is no love. Plus the request was again inappropriate as previously analyzed. It's important to remember that *"The strongest negotiating position is always being able to walk away and mean it."* as stated by Michael Yon).

Yana replies to him: *"Fjodar... We have already*

talked about that. I have already been extremely clear in person. There is no need to repeat it again.. I wish you a good evening.".

A thirty minutes later arrives another message: *"I am a friend of Fjodar. Fjodar is drunk and I brought him home. Sorry that he disturbed you. Good evening to you too".*

Yana: *"I understand. Hopefully Fjodar will get well soon, but it doesn't change what I meant to say. Please keep this message on his phone so he can read it later. Good evening again".*

(When a person is drunk, his/her decisions making can be influenced by the drunkness. The drunkness removes any kind of self-imposed inhibitions, it clouds the judgment of the individual and it can cause the person to make rash decisions and actions.)

A few hours later, Essenia arrives. Yana warmly welcome her home, and shows to her Fjodar messages. They laugh a bit about the situation, and then Yana shows to Essenia the book.

Yana: *"I started to read it, it is very interesting".*
Essenia reads the first pages: *"Indeed. Where did Fjodar order it? I should get a copy too".*
Yana: *"I will give you all the details right now".*
Yana gives to Essenia a paper with the title of the book and the details. After having seen some pages of the book and got the details, Essenia and Yana start to talk about something else as Yana cookes some pelmeni and later they have dinner.

Four days later, Diego calls again Yana to fix a new definite date for the following week. Yana is looking forward to meeting Diego again, so they agree on the details and wish to each other an amazing day.

(**The man usually has to do a minimal effort in the beginning of the dating process by contacting the girl once for week until she feels comfortable enough to contact him first in less than a week. When her attraction is high enough, usually after a few dates she will start to contact the man in less than a week, increasing the frequency of contact as her attraction grows. At that point the man can simply back off, wait to hear from her and when she *"puts herself in the orbit"* by initiating contact, express that he is happy to hear from her and planning a new date by asking when she is free to meet up. If the woman complains about the man not writing to her first despite the fact that she is chasing, then the man can simply stick to initiate a once for week contact. However after the chasing starts by the woman's part if the man initiates contact for more than 20-30% of the time, the woman attraction will slowly drop. We will talk more about the chasing mechanism later.**)

The days pass and it is time for the second date between Diego and Yana. They meet at the agreed place – "Potsuelev most" ("The bridge of kisses") and warmly greet each other.

(**The *"bridge of kisses"* is one of the most romantic places in the whole city of Saint Petersburg. Often couples come here and put locks there with their initials on it as a symbolic reminder of their relationships. It also has an amazing view of the Moyka river and it is possible to see the GUAP university from the bridge: it is the big yellow structure in Balshaja Morskaja street, close to the river**).

The first place they go this time is to have some drinks.

Diego as usual lets Yana to talk 70-80% of the time, as he did already in the first date.

Yana: *"I am having a great time with you"*.

Diego: *"Me too"*.

(As women tend to be usually more driven by emotions, they will link how they feel around the man to the presence of that man. A date is supposed to be a great occasion to have fun and spend amazing time together, not to be each other's therapist.)

After having had some drinks, at the exit of the club they start to make out and then go for a walk, in which Yana starts to take Diego by hand, intertwining her fingers with his fingers.

(When a date flows in different places, each place feels like an additional date to the woman. This usually speeds up the seduction process. Taking another person by hand while also intertwining fingers with him/her is usually a body language's signal indicating a strong sexual desire towards the other person).

They enjoy the great and romantic view and they start to make out more heavily and affectionate.

Diego says in a moment of pause: *"Yana, what about we grab a bottle of wine and we go to my place to better enjoy each other?"*.

Yana: *"I'm not ready yet"*.

Diego keeps acting cool and says: *"Okay, then let's hang out some more."*

(Kissing leads to make out, making out to heavy petting and affection. This in turn leads to the suggestion of going somewhere else more privately, usually initiated by the man. If the man invites her to go somewhere else more private and the woman doesn't feel ready, the man should keep acting cool and wait one hour or so and when the situation is again more passional he can try again. If the man acts unglued when the first offer is turned down, then he shoots himself in the foot as with women is needed infinite patience. Usually at the second try in an hour or so when the situation is more passional again, the woman should be enough warmed up and say yes to the offer).

They go and sit to a closer park. Here they talk some more and the heavy petting restarts. As it passes an hour or so, this time is Yana suggesting to go to her place: *"Diego, would you like to come at my place for a cup of tea?"*.
Diego: *"Sure, with pleasure. Let's go"*.

(When a woman feels ready and warm enough, she might even take the initiative to invite the man to a more private place. This happens especially when she has high attraction and a direct type of personality.)

Diego and Yana arrive to Yana's house.
As soon as they enter, Pallino greets Yana and curiously comes to see the guest.

Diego: *"Hi Pallino!"*

Pallino starts to affectionately indicate wanting to be caressed by Diego - *"What an affectionate cat!"* he comments as he caress the cat.

Yana: "*Usually he is quite diffident around new people. It's cool that he immediately liked you. That said, feel yourself like you were at home*".

Diego: *"Thank you"*.

Yana: *"I will prepare some green tea for you and some black tea for me. Feel free to sit down and relax, I will show you fully the house later".*

They drink, relax and then Yana shows to him the house. Then they sit more comfortably in her bed to talk a bit. And as they do so, they start to kiss again with passion. After a few minutes, Yana starts to hold back and Diego stops, so they start to talk again. Then a few minutes later, they start to kiss again with even more passion as Diego starts to play with her hair. Then again she feels the need to back off a bit, so Diego backs off again and they continue to talk. Then they kiss again and this time Diego also massages gently her neck from behind as they kiss. **(This is a *"two step forward and one step backward"* mentality. The man slowly pushes the situation forward alongside with a *"take it or leave it"* attitude by not getting attached to the outcome of sex and letting the woman gradually warm up building anticipation in the seduction process. When the man feels a resistence by the woman, it's simply a signal for the man to slow down the process a bit by backing off and waiting a few minutes to restart pushing through her barriers step by step).**

Diego and Yana continue like this and every time a piece of cloth goes down.

Yana: *"I don't usually do this in the second date".*

Diego playfully says: *"Is that written in your rule book? You better throw that away, because it doesn't work on me. I know that you want me, so bring those beautiful lips over here and kiss me with even more passion".*

Yana smiles and comes to Diego with even more passion. (**Always look at what a woman does and her emotional status in the present moment: this is the key to understand women. In this case, lines like** *"I don't usually do this so fast"* **etc.. are usually simply an automatic** *"anti-slut"* **defense, as most women deep down are afraid to be labelled as sluts when they engage in sexual activities with a new man. But looking at the her actions here, the woman is there enjoying the moment and coming more passionately to the man – in this case her words could be translated in** *"I'm open to have sex with you, but I don't want responsability in this"*... **Sex should be the man's fault.**)

Eventually they are so turned on that all her clothes go down and as Diego removes his last ones forming a love glove, they finally hook up.

(**In the moment the woman feels fully comfortable and is emotionally open, the man succeeds in breaking her barriers as she feels totally safe to hook up with him. It's not a coincidence that a lot of women love to say:** *"...and it just happened"* **when talking to their girl friends about these kind of situations. Masculine energy afterall is about logic, purpose, leadership and breaking barriers, while feminine energy is more emotional, connection based and about opening to receive love. The man penetrates the woman in every way (mentally, physically, emotionally and spiritually) as the woman slowly opens up to him more and more as she feels ready and receptive.**

During foreplay, when giving oral sex to a woman, the man should wait a bit before entering in her – this will drive the woman completely nuts with pleasure. When a woman says: *"I want you to cum* *now"* it usually boils down to two main possibilities.

The first is a subtle test to feel the strenght of the man. In this case, if the man waits at least a few minutes to cum for her – the anticipation will build up even more to the point that she might come several times in a row until the man gives her the finish on his own terms. This subtle test is designated so that she feels completely safe in the fact that the man can have completely his way with her and she will be still safe and protected by him.

The second is that the man might be doing some wrong moves and so the woman is not fully satisfied of what's happening. When this situation arises, the woman will become distracted, or she will try to get the man go in a different direction or rushing towards the conclusion as she doesn't feel fully satisfied in how it is going. In this case, it's a good idea to ask her quality questions about how she likes to be sexually pleased as every woman has her own unique tastes in sexual activities and then act accordingly to her feedback.)

After a night of passion, the two wake in the morning with Pallino asking for food as Diego is holding her hard and she is relaxed in his arms.

(Holding hard the other person in a hug is a masculine trait, relaxing on the body of the one who holds hard a feminine trait).

They have breakfast, then Diego dresses up and needs to go as he has a business meeting. They greet each other with a kiss and wishing to each other an amazing day.

CHASING

The day after the second date with Diego, Essenia and Yana meets up.

"Diego is incredible, we had such a magical and amazing evening." says Yana to Essenia.

"Did you two hook up?" asks with curiosity Essenia with a smirk in her face.

"Yes, it just happened... Not only he is a true gentleman, but also a great lover" replies Yana to her.

"Great, I'm happy for you!" says Essenia to her.

(A woman has 3 great conflicts in her mind.

The first is the *"conflict of time"*: a woman might choose to invest time in a specific man to model him in the ideal man that she wishes to have as partner, or either she tests as much men as possible in the search for that ideal partner.

The second is the *"conflict of sex"*: a woman might either be more conservative thus needing more time to open to the experience of sex and so she waits more to hook up with a man – or she doesn't give sex such an high value and importance so she will hook up faster.

The third is the *"conflict of relationships"*: a woman might either focus on a more idealistic of them viewing for example herself like a disney princess etc... Or be far more focused on the realistic sides of a relationship.

The combination of the 3 factors will influence her behaviour, thus influencing in turn the flow and the timing of events and situations during dating and relationships.)

Yana is thinking more and more about the date with Diego.

The third day after the date, she decides to message him: *"The other date was amazing Diego. I can't wait to see you again"*.

A bit later a message from Diego arrives: *"It's great to hear from you Yana! Yeah it was amazing and I would love to see you again. When are you free to meet up?"*.

Yana's eyes light up at the message: *"Next week I have a lot of free time"*.

Diego replies: *"Great, next week there is an interesting cultural festival in the evening. I will send now a photo with the details, let's meet in the front door 10 minutes before the beginning of the festival."* - *** _photo sent_ *** - *"Sounds good?"*.

Yana: *"Great, I'm free on that day and hour. it sounds cool. See you there, look forward to it!"*.

Diego: *"Likewise, can't wait to meet you again. Have an amazing day"*.

Yana: *"Thanks, you too!"*.

(When the attraction of the woman is high enough, she will start to reach out in less than a week. This is called "*chasing*" and is a feminine trait. The four horsemen of chasing are: 1) mystery, 2) emotional rollercoaster, 3) investment, 4) anticipation.

Mystery causes women to wonder about the man, and it's scientifically proven that women are more attracted to men whose feelings are unclear. The more a woman thinks and wonders about the man when the man is not physically present around her, the more her attraction rises.

As this happens, the woman is going to experience emotional storms. This bring to the second factor:

emotional rollercoaster. Since women tend to be driven by emotions, the higher the emotional rollercoaster and the more they become addicted to it. Essentially the woman wants to be the protagonist of her own personal soap opera.

This leads to investment. The woman will invest more and more in the frequentation, by actively initiating contact herself in less than a week. Usually this happens after a few dates. Although in rare cases the woman might have a very high level of interest to begin with, in which case she will invite the man to meet up by herself and chase him from the beginning: when this happens, things are as easiest as it can be.

The final factor is anticipation. The more she anticipates and wonders what is going to happen, the more her attraction and effort grows and so the cycle repeats again, again and again...).

A few minutes later, Yana's phone rings: her dad Vladimir is calling.

Yana: *"Hi dad!"*.

Vladimir: *"Hi sweetheart! What's up?"*.

Yana: *"I'm great, thanks! You?"*.

Vladimir: *"Great, thanks! Remember the favour that you asked me a week ago? I finally completed all the preparations, so feel free to retire the material whenever you want"*.

Yana: *"Amazing! Thank you very much dad, you are a life saver. Can I retire it right now? It would be very useful for tomorrow at work"*.

Vladimir: *"Yeah, sure. See you later dear"*.

Yana: *"See you later!"*.

As Yana is going to her parents' house, she notices a little girl crying with her dad calming her down and soon after the girl starts to smile again.

(Women are pre-programmed since childhood to pursue the presence of a masculine presence. When women are little girls, the main masculine presence in their life is their father. When they become an adult, the main masculine presence will become the man that they love. Every person has both masculine and feminine energy: with masculine being more about logic, purpose and breaking barriers, and feminine being more about emotion, connection and opening up to receive love. The goal is to be able to use both energies as needed, while fully owning your main core.

We can picture the masculine energy as a mountain and the feminine energy as wind. No matter what the wind does, the mountain is there and it's not even scratched by it. And if the wind is temporarily absent, the mountain doesn't start to walk around searching where is the wind. Thus chasing is a feminine trait.

Smart men know this and only do an initial effort of once for week to plan a date when the attraction of the woman is still not high enough for her to actively chase the man by reaching out in less than a week.

When she starts to chase, the man should simply back off and wait to hear from her, appreciate the message and plan the next definite date. The higher the attraction she feels, the more she will chase the man and if she is chasing the man, she can't dump him. If despite chasing, she complains about the man not writing first anymore – then it's okay to stick to initiate contact with her once for week. The man is the leader and the mountain of dating and relationships, thus providing the possibility to the woman to fully relax in her femininity just for him. The natural sexual polarity for dating and relationships is masculine man and feminine woman. In 10% or less of the couples, we can notice that a reversal - masculine woman and feminine man which is greatly supported by feminists and often portrayed in medias etc.. but it's not the natural and standard sexual polarity. Trying to force this in a standard situation of masculine man plus feminine woman couple leads only to misery and depolarization, which cause the loss of attraction and passion on the longer term).

Yana arrives to her parent's house, greets her dad Vladimir and her mother Liubov. She talks a bit, gets the material and then she has to go – so she greets them and goes to see with an old friend of hers. Her name is Irina, she casually bumped into her some weeks ago after some years since she last saw her, so Yana invited her for a drink.
As they are talking, Irina's phone rings.
Irina: *"Sorry Yana, I have to take the call. Wait a minute"*. As Irina replies, Yana could her a man screaming in a needy and complaining manner:
"You disappeared suddenly. I sent you so many sweet messages these past few days, you read them and you didn't write me even an hi! Why? What's happening???".
Irina: *"I'm sorry Bob. It's not you, it's me. I need to write a new page of my life. I'm not interested in continue dating you, I wish you all the best"* and Irina closes the phone.

Irina explains to Yana that was Bob that called here right now, they dated a few weeks but then he started to get super needy and she got tired of it.

(This man has fallen under the *"illusion of action"* trap. He forgot than an action is simply a mean to an end, so when doing something it's important to keep in mind the big picture and the wished end result. At that point if the action is beneficial in order to get the desired result then do it, otherwise don't do it. Acting simply for the sake of action without keeping in mind the goal and the big picture is *"illusion of action"*. An example is when a person starts to water a rose far more than the needed amount, hoping that this causes the rose to grow faster than its natural timing of growth.

Not only the rose doesn't grow faster in this way, but rather the rose dies due to excessive watering.

In this case the illusion of action of the man was motivated by the *"need to do something to make her like him more"*. In truth nature has already the attraction part covered, so there is no need to rush the flow of it. Either there is mutual attraction or there isn't, if there is then it still takes time for it to become stronger – exactly like a caterpillar takes time to gradually become a butterfly and if the process it is forced, the animal dies.

In the same way, if the process is forced in the hope of fastening it, the attraction is slowly ruined. When the man initiates more than 20-30% of the contact after that the woman has started to chase, her attraction will slowly lower over time and she will start to back off more and more. This happens because chasing is a feminine trait, so by chasing actively the woman - the man basically becomes the feminine pole in the frequentation. This in turn forces the woman to become the masculine pole in the frequentation in order to try to balance the sexual polarity, however usually women don't like to be in their masculine essence and so this causes a depolarization process over time. When the man starts to overpursue, he has a shot to turn the situation around by backing off and letting her to reach out first. As that say recitates:

"Sometimes the best way to get someone's attention is to remove yours". **Another example is music, if there was no space between the notes then it would be noise instead. That said, if he doesn't back off until she hears from her and he continues with the overpursuing, she will eventually lose all her respect and attraction towards him, at which point it's only a matter of time until she blows him off by saying something alongside the lines of** *"it's not you, it's me."* **(**underline**translation** = *"it's you, but I don't want to hurt so I say it's me"*)**,** *"I need a pause.","it's time for me to write a new page of my life"* **and similar break up/blown-off lines** *)*.

As Yana replays the conversation of Irina with Bob, Igor suddenly comes back to his mind. She remembers how the last conversation with him was heated argument which degenerated in the break up.

(Never argue with a woman. As women tend to be driven by emotion, an argument will cause her to simply build up more emotional charge and spill it around in an explosive manner and/or with hasty generalizations.

A woman rather wants either: 1) to be opened up emotionally or 2) to be put in her place when she acts in a disrespectful way. Both tests are designed to feel the masculine strength of the man, thus returning in her femininity for him.

The first scenario is usually deployed by the usage of silence to conceal her pain and it is easy noticeable when the woman says *"I'm fine"* **when looking at her it's obvious that she is lying. In this case, the woman is testing if the man truly cares enough about her with actions to open her up and listens properly to her and her emotional status. If the man ignores this, the woman will get angry at him: for example the woman**

might suddendly shout at him to do something like throwing away the garbage, and after that she is still angry at him – bottom line is that she wants to be opened emotionally and if the man doesn't make an effort to do that then she will act more and more bitchy as she feels that the man doesn't care and that he is acting weak, thus forcing her to enter in her masculine side which she doesn't like. The correct way to pass this test is simple. When the woman says *"I'm fine"* and by looking at her it's obvious that she is not fine, the man should focus on making clear that the woman is not feeling fine and that he wants to know what's troubling her. With masculine presence, touch and humour he must stay there and persist until she starts to say what's troubling her. It might take a bit of time but eventually she will break down and start to talk, when she does the man should encourage her to tell everything and letting her know that he is listening properly by repeating portions of what she says to him and correlating that to her emotional status, letting her ventilate completely. At that point the man can do a quick recap about what happened related to her feelings and if needed a proper apologize on the lines of: *"By doing this you felt like that and by saying this you felt like that other way... I should had done this other way so that you felt appreciated... I'm sorry."*

After this, the woman will feel relieved and lightened up, saying things on the line of: *"Thanks so much for having talked!!"*, *"I feel so much better now"*, *"I was just emotional"* etc...   and she will be again fully relaxed in her femininity for the man.

In the second case, when the woman acts disrespectfully – she simply wants to be put in her place. She wants to feel the masculine strength of the man by seeing him standing up for himself. If the man doesn't stand up for himself, then the woman subconsciously questions his strenght and skill in protecting her if she is in danger. This has also deep evolutionary reasons, as men usually are stronger than women plus women are very vulnerable during the phase of pregnancy. Also love is based on respect and the only way to fully own the heart of a woman is if she knows that the man will stand up for himself and if needed he will walk away from her when she messes with his healthy boundaries to the point of no-return. The man's purpose in life should always come first. That's why for example when a soldier goes to war and his woman says to him not to go - she will still appreciate him more if he goes to war instead as the soldier's purpose is to go in war to protect what's dear to him. By focusing on his purpose, the man alignes with his masculinity and exudes a masculine vibe. Being an alpha is about fully owning and be comfortable in your main core. For a man the main core is masculine, while for a woman instead the main core is the feminine one.)

Irina and Yana start to talk about more fun topics and after a while Yana has to go, so she greets her and returns home to feed Pallino.

Yana now thinks often about Diego and writes to him more and more, as they continue to hang around, have fun and hook up.

(The higher the attraction, the more she will initiate contact as she is chasing. By week 7+, if the man does everything correctly, she enters in the *"love phase"* in which she will usually contact at least once daily – everything women do is to be appreciated and when she is in love, she wants the attention of her man all the time).

A WEEK OF SILENCE

7 weeks of dating passed by and Diego thinks more and more often about Yana.

Diego and Emilio go for a drink at the end of a business event and start to talk about Yana and Essenia.

Diego: *"Yana is amazing. We are dating and she started to write to me pretty much every day. The last few days she went into silent mode."*

Emilio: *"It's most likely just a test to see how you react when she doesn't reach out to you."*

Diego: *"Yes, I think so as well. Women love to bluff and will always test men when they feel attraction. How is going with Essenia? Have you heard from her?"*

Emilio: *"Time ago I tried to schedule a definite date with Essenia but she didn't seem enthusiastic about it. Her attitude was kind of <<eh, maybe>>. So I withdrawed the offer, telling her to contact me when she figured her schedule and since then I haven't heard anything from her."*

Diego: *"I see... It's her loss"*.

Emilio: *"Yeah, indeed"*.

(Most men are clueless in various levels of degree about women and their fundamental mistake is trying to project logic and attraction on women and giving too much weight to women's words. These clueless men don't realize the simple truth that women tend to be more driven by emotions. Women are totally rational when you understand where they come from: the women's operative system is emotionally based, rather than logical. Therefore to fully understand women, the key is to look at her actions, the clues that she sends to men and her emotional status in the present moment and then act accordingly. On average in a group of 100 men, the number of alpha men can be literally counted within the fingers of a hand. Therefore, the best choice for a man in dating and relationships scene is to fully own his masculine core and understanding how attraction works exactly, thus becoming an alpha man and giving him the best possible shot with any woman who feels attraction towards him. It's easy to spot her level of attraction by noticing the clues she sends and how she acts around the man: her body language, if she asks personal questions and especially inquiring if you have a girlfriend (high signal of interest) etc..

When you are an alpha man, you literally don't have a competition as *"scarcity creates value"* and women are pre-programmed since childhood to pursue the most dominant man in their respective eyes, plus clueless men will eventually screw themselves up by making sooner or later different kinds of unnecessary mistakes that ruin attraction. As a result of this, as alpha man you naturally develop an *"abundance mentality"* and you are always one step ahead, knowing what to do and what not to do in any given moment and situation. Dating is a numbers' game: some will like you, some will not. Sometimes even by doing everything correctly, an alpha man can still be rejected and in this case rejection is seen as *"it's her loss"* rather than a personal loss of the man).

Several days pass by and Yana still doesn't write or call, but Diego calls the bluff and sticks to silence as well.

(As a proverb says: *"Sometimes the best way to get someone's attention is to remove yours"*).

On the 7th day of silence, Yana breaks it with a message: *"You are my one in a million."*.

Diego is very pleased by the message and replies: *"Me too, Yana"* and enthusiastically plans with her a new date.

Diego called her bluff correctly and brilliantly passes her *"week of silence"* test.

(As the woman is approaching the *"I love you"* moment, she gets more and more affectionate. Usually the *"I love you"* phase starts around week 7+ of dating, but before moving fully to the *"I love you"* moment, most women do a test to see if the man knows that *"You must love a person in a way that the person you love feels free"*.

The test consists in disappearing for roughly a week even if everything is going absolutely great. No call, no messages, no mail, no sms – absolutely nothing. A woman does this test to see how the man reacts and if she can get a rise out of him.

If the man starts to act unglued and reaches out to her in argumentative manner, the man fails the test and she will back off more and more. Most clueless men when faced with this test will contact her in an unglued way, trying to argue with her, acting needy and continuing to persist instead to do what they should – back off a bit and respect her space. If they continue doing that way, the woman will feel less and less comfortable about him until the woman gives the *"it's not you, it's me"* break up/blown off line treatment or similar ones.

If the man waits a week, at that point either she writes first or he can ask in a calm way how she is doing, then in this case he passes the test and she will be even more affectionate to him than before.)

ESCLUSIVITY

Diego and Yana meet up. Yana arrives with a stunning dress and hair style.

Diego: *"You look amazing Yana! Stunning dress."*

Yana: *"I want to look more beautiful for you."*

Diego: *"Thanks, I appreciate dear. Let's go."*

Diego leads Yana to a cool place.

(When a woman feels relaxed in her femininity around the leadership of the man, she will take a great care of her looks. She will usually keep her hair longer and she will take a great care of her dressing style. She might also colour her nails and wear make up, depending on her taste and likes.

She does this both for herself and also to impress the man, as the man opened her up especially for him. Everything a woman does is about being noticed. When a woman is in love - she wants the man's attention all the time.

That's why a woman will call or message the man during the day: she does that to let him know that she cares about him and she is thinking about him. A good rule of thumb for men is to appreciate the woman's call, telling her that it's very sweet by her part to contact you during the day to show how much she cares and that you will see her later – and when you see her, give her your full presence and attention as reward. Instead when depolarization happens, we can notice that the woman stops taking care of her appearance, she tends to keep her hair shorter and assume the leadership position by walking in front of the man while keeping a bitchy face. She is resentful about the weakness of the man she chose and you can notice the man is feeling miserable about it. Often these couples wear the same clothes and by looking at them you can notice how they slowly become colder and more distant towards each other.

If the depolarization continues, at that point it's usually only a matter of time until there is a break-up between them or alternatively the couple stays together *"just for the kids"* but with the passion being completely gone. Staying *"just for kids"* however it sets a bad example for the kids as during childhood they will subconsciously correlate a loving relationship with how they see their parents behaving towards each other and thus when they enter in dating phase, they will subconsciously choose partners that replicate the behavioral relationship pattern of their parents and continue to do so until the person in question realizes this fact and break the vicious circle).

Suddenly Yana asks Diego: *"Where is this going?"*.

Diego playfully asks: *"What do you mean?"*.

Yana: *"I love you and I want you all for myself"*.

Diego: *"I love you too! So are you saying that you want to be in an exclusive relationship, that's what you mean?"*.

Yana: *"Yes, you are absolutely amazing. I want you to be my boyfriend"*.

Diego: *"Great, I'm up for it. It's settled"*.

And then Diego kisses Yana with passion.

(When the woman is ready, she will bring the topic of wanting to be exclusive with the man. It usually happens by week 7+. It is always better that women brings up the labels, as women fall in love slower over time. When all the signals are there and she is ready, she will say something on the lines: *"where is this going?"*, *"I want you all for myself"*, *"when are we going to live together?"*, *"when are we going to marry?"* etc...

When she asks that, the man can playfully say *"what do you mean?"* and she will confirm that she wants to be exclusive with him.

About the *"I love you"* magic words: it's usually better to let the woman say them first and then the man can replicate if it's mutual.

Also the man shouldn't bring exclusivity or relationships label up. If the man asks her to be his girlfriend, then he rushes the flow of frequentation and deep down the situation would feel forced to the woman - even in the case that she agrees at first about being exclusive, she might easily turn flaky later on as the idea of being exclusive wasn't initiated by her in the first place.

When the woman asks for exclusivity, either the request can be agreed in which case it's important to remember that you go in a relationship to give and wanting the other person to grow in a better version of themselves. Or alternatively if the man wants to keep the thing in a more casual tone then he can say to her something on the lines of: *"You should keep your options open and if you find someone to be in relationship with, then go for it. In the meanwhile let's just enjoy each other and see what happens."*).

As they continue with the date, a woman passing close to them is approached by a clueless man. The man first uses an inauthentic pick up line and then he asks her if she has a boyfriend. The woman looks at him in a disinterested fashion and tell him to go away.

(A common mistake I noticed many men do is asking a woman: *"Do you have a boyfriend?"*. This is a huge mistake because first of all, it sets a weird vibe in the air – more precisely about wanting to lock her out in a commitment without having knew her at all and besides that only women are allowed to bring labels up when they feel ready.

Secondly, the question is unnecessary. When the man sees a desirable woman and he wants to know her availability towards him, he should simply look at her in the eyes and smile, then looking at her reaction.

If a woman is interested. available and ready to flirt, she will send signals of attraction like smiling, looking down when you look at her, submissive body language, playing with her hair etc when you look at her.

Only the woman knows exactly her background situation: she might not seeing anyone, she might be dating someone and still not being exclusive with anyone or she might have a boyfriend that she is breaking up with but first she is looking up for a replacement. Some women will look for a replacement before breaking up with the current boyfriend that they have decided to leave – that's why for example when a marriage ends, sometimes the woman after a week is already with another man leaving most men puzzled about that – while the explanation is very simple. She was obviously already seeing this other dude during the relationship with her husband, and waited the end of it to showcase him around more freely. An alpha man knows well that when the woman feels ready to be exclusive, in the moment that he becomes her mountain then she will blown off all the other possible admirers in the picture as she bring the topic of being exclusive and he agrees with it.

If a woman is in an exclusive and fulfilling relationship, not emotionally available and/or not interested, then she will not look back and smile when the man looks at her, she will not send any signal of attraction and she will treat the man as if he were invisible to her eyes. So in this case, the man should avoid to approach or to spend time flirting with her.

It's amazing how much information a woman sends around all the time and sometimes she is not even aware of this fact. By observing carefully what a woman does, her body language and how she acts around others then the man can easily notice and pinpoint a lot about her).

Returning to Diego and Yana, they are having a great time together. After seeing a cool and romantic place, they go to Diego's house in which they passionately spent the night together.

The following day, Yana calls Essenia: *"Essenia, big news! Big news!"*.

Essenia: *"What it is?"*.

Yana: *"Diego is officially my boyfriend !!!"*.

Essenia: *"Great, I'm happy for you!"*.

Yana: *"Diego is absolutely incredible. I'm going to tell you all the details in person. Are you free this afternoon?"*.

Essenia: *"Yeah, sure!"*.

Yana: *"Then come at my place at 16:30 for a tea and I'll tell you better."*.

Yana and Essenia meet up and Yana tells her better what happened: Essenia is very glad for Yana.

THE DISCIPLINE OF LOVE

A few months passed since the evening in which Yana bringed up the exclusivity topic and Diego agreed. Their relationship is going great. Diego continues to court her as he knows well that *"Courtship never ends"* plus he also ensures to communicate with her properly all the time, by putting her in her place when is needed and opening her up as necessary.

(Most men, when entering into an exclusive relationship, commit two big mistakes.

The first is to get complacent, mistakenly thinking that since they are in an exclusive relationship, there is no longer need to court the woman. It's important to always keep gauging her attraction and reading her signals and actions, always continuing to court her in an unpredictable manner. When going out in a date, don't always go the same day of the week, same places and with the same routine every time: it will kill all the mystery and anticipation.

Another great advice is to randomly put some dedication cards/stickers with messages of appreciation towards the woman somewhere where she can find it, but not always in the same place and with different timing.

Other great idea is from to time to bring her flowers as gift but don't do that when you have a serious talk or to apologize, as the flowers would not feel an authentic gift of appreciation from your heart.

Bottom line, the main idea is to keep her wondering: "*what is he going to do next?*" etc...

To make the courtship even more effective, one should

make sure to find out which love language the partner uses and to stick with doing more actions that matches the love language the other person uses: in this way the partner will feel better your love towards him/her. There is a great book called "*The 5 love languages*" of Gary Chapman that deeply explores this. In a nutshell there are 5 languages and every person tends to have an higher affinity especially with one of them:

-"*Words of affection*" (<u>feeling love by encouragement, listening and appreciation</u>): Do unexpected compliments, cards, texts and appreciate the partner often. Avoid non-constructive criticism and not-appreciative behaviour towards the partner's efforts.

-"*Physical touch*" (<u>feeling love due to physical contact</u>): in this case it's important to focus a lot in physical contact – hug, kisses, hold hands regularly and making intimacy a priority. Avoid physical neglect, long periods without intimacy and cold behaviour towards your partner.

-"*Receiving gifts*" (<u>feeling love by seeing that your partner is making you a priority and showing that with purposfulness</u>): give thoughtful gifts and gestures, putting a lot of emphasis on small things as to your partner they will matter a lot and always express gratitude when receiving a gift from him/her. Avoid forgetting special occasions and being unenthusiastic when receiving a gift from him/her.

-"*Quality time*" (<u>feeling love by presence and focused attention</u>): in this case, it is essential to focus on creating special moments together, take walks and do small things for your partner – occasions like going out somewhere for a weekend together are a huge bonus. Avoid distractions when spending time together, long periods without one-on-one and being unappreciative of your partner's presence.

-"*Acts of service*" (feeling love by teamwork in the relationship): in this case, your partner puts a great focus on treating the relationship like a team partnership – so do chores together, make them breakfast in bed, go out of your way to help alleviate your partner's daily schedule and workload. Avoid making the requests of others a more important priority and lacking follow up on tasks whatever they are big or small.

If a man stops courting her woman, then the woman over the course of time will become more and more bitchy about it. She might tollerate the situation at first for a while, but then she will start to complain and to send hints of not being happy about how the relationship is going. If those signals are being kept ignored by the man, then in the end it's only a matter of time before than someone else will court her instead and she will break up with him. Bottom line: courtship never ends so both partner should make an effort in this and not getting complacent, with the man leading the process and the woman being open to it.

The second biggest mistake that most men do when they enter in a relationship is not communicating properly with the woman. As said previously, a man should never argue logically with a woman as woman tend to be more driven by emotions and thus arguing will simply make her spill around more and more emotion. In truth she wants either to be opened up emotionally when she is not feeling okay or to be put in her place when she behaves disrespectfully.

This is an important point to notice: women usually resolve a problem by talking with others as they are more emotionally driven and by talking they discharge away the emotional stress and weight they feel inside. Men instead usually prefer to retire in their cave and think for practical solution by themselves, as men tend to be more logically driven. So when a woman sees that her man is having trouble. she should state that she is there for him and point out if he needs to have some alone time to think in his man-cave: the man will greatly appreciate this and after he has finished thinking about the matter, he will return in a very appreciative mood and fully focused on the woman. About communication, think before saying something to the partner by putting in the partner's shoes and keep in mind the love languages too. So if you and your partner use different love languages, make sure to make a mutual effort to see things from his/her perspective and love language view and if it's possible be open to find a compromise to make everyone happy about the situation. Sometimes miscommunication can happen because a partner feels loved more in a certain way and the other in another way, and they don't make an effort in seeing things from the other person perspective and act accordingly. In a relationship, open your heart to your partner and don't hold back, be appreciative of your partner's presence. If you are the man, be her mountain: no matter what happens and how much she might test you, you are the leader of the relationship and nothings shakes you. If you are the woman, be playful and relaxed in your femininity for him. That's the natural standard sexual polarity: masculine man and feminine woman. The opposite can also work: feminine man plus masculine woman, however it's rare and an exception to the rule. And talking about gay and lesbian couples: the more masculine partner will be "*the man*" of the frequentation while the more feminine will be "*the woman*"of the couple, thus forming sexual polarity).

One night Yana tries to test Diego. She says to Diego that she had an erotic dream involving her and an handsome model in her work enviroment.

Diego didn't get mad about that and says to her: *"Then what about you come over here and show this dream to me?"*.

She giggled and they had a very passional night.

(In this occasion the woman tried to test if she could get a rise out of him by talking about another man.

He passed the test by remaining calm and centered in his masculinity: she tried to see if he would get jealous and he didn't, thus making her feel safe and relaxed in her femininity again for him and he becomes the protagonist of the erotic dream that she had. Jealousy is not love: jealousy is a toxic and negative feeling due to a sense of inferiority and possessivity, treating the partner like an object instead that a person. People are meant to be loved and object to be used, not the other way around. People are not object that you can claim possess of.

You go into relationship to give and wanting the other person to grow into a better version of themself. Authentic healthy loving relationship are about sharing your completeness and happiness with your partner, trusting your partner and respecting his/her individual freedom. After all love is freedom and freedom is the natural status of every living being, therefore *"You must love in such a way that the other person feels free"*. Therefore in an authentic loving relationship, there is no place for jealousy, lack of trust and disrespect to begin with. Relationships that are based on negative traits like possessivity, disrespect

and lack of trust are toxic relationships. In this kind of relationships, the two person completely emotionally depend of each other like a parasite from the host – so instead of going there to give and to share completeness, they focus on what they can get from the other person. Bottom line – toxic relationships are not an authentic relationship, but rather a transaction.

Sometimes a person might ignore the red flags of a toxic person and enter into a relationship. A common example is when a person ignores the red flag of a toxic person with cluster B type of personality (narcissists, psychopaths, histrionics).

Cluster B people love to pair with people that have trouble in putting healthy boundaries. A narcissist is concerned all about boosting his/her ego by the means of adulation of others but in truth he/she feels like shit inside. It's interesting to notice that narcissistic women tend to do an incredible amount of selfies and post them in their social profile because they are seeking likes as a form of online supply of adulation to boost their ego. Psychopaths and histrionics have similar tendencies, except that psychopaths' endgame is more about control, destruction and power and they tend to have an high impulsivity, while for histrionics is all about being the star of any situation and the adulation over everything else. A common tendency all the cluster B share is their relational pattern: "*elevation*", "*delevation*" and "*discard*".

In the first phase *"elevation"* the cluster B starts quickly to treat the other person like the king/queen of the world etc... People that suffer from low self-esteem are more likely to fall prey of this trick.

When the target falls for the cluster B, the cluster B moves to *"delevation"*... basically in the eyes of the cluster B everything becomes the other person's fault.

If the person doesn't stand up for himself/herself then the cluster B will eventually move to *"discard"* phase by disappearing and stonewalling any attempt of communication, leaving often the target confused about what happened. As soon as you spot the cluster B behavioral patterns in a potential partner, I strongly advice you to run like hell and never look back, ideally before getting emotionally attached. Cluster B are not suitable candidates for authentic relationships as it's all about them and their endgame).

Sometimes Yana asks to Diego when she gets a new dress about if it makes her look fat.

Diego replies: *"Honey I will tell you what I find really sexy. It's you training naked with me in martial arts. That would be really sexy"*.

At which Yana smiles and Diego sometimes teases her when he is go to training: *"Why don't you come to train naked with me in martial arts? I told you that it would be very sexy"* with her giggling in response.

(When a woman asks things like: *"Does this make me look fat?"* and similar – these are loaded questions. The best answer to these questions is neither a *"yes"* or a *"no"*, but rather a playful banter combined with a genuine compliment, like the one above).

As Diego needs to focus on a long series of negotiation about his business for at least a week, he promises to Yana to pass quality one-on-one time after this deal is completed. Yana understands and wishes him good luck. 3 days after this Yana goes out with friends and she gets drunk. When she gets home, she receives an unexpected message...

AN UNEXPECTED MESSAGE

....Yana opens the message and she is shocked at reading it: *"Hi Yana, it has been a while. I'm sorry for having behaved like an asshole towards you. I would like to see you again and rekindle things. If you are interested, let me know when you are free in order to plan a definite date... Igor"*.

Since the break up, they never bumped into each other.

A strong flow of emotions and memories starts to erupt in Yana: both the amazing moment with Igor (great dates, the passional nights, etc...) but also the fierce arguments, the communication problems and the scene of the break up.

(When talking about getting an ex back, this desire usually happens when we have a situation involving a dumper and a dumped. The dumper is the one that initiate and lead the break up, while the dumped is the one who doesn't agree with breaking up.

In these kinds of situation, sometimes happens that one of them propose to the other the possibility of being *"just friends"*. Most commonly this is offered by the woman in order to trying reduce the emotional damage of the break up. However agreeing on being just friends with an ex will lower his/her attraction towards you – because if you want to get back with an ex, you should apply Michael Yon's principle of negotiation: *"The strongest negotiating position is always being able to walk away and mean it."*. If you want to get an ex back, you should never agree on being friends only.

Thus we can distinguish two main cases:

-*DUMPER*: A dumper is in a stronger starting position. If you are the dumper, this allows you to ask once forgiveness for the pain caused by the break up and offering a date to the dumped. If the dumped is willing to go to in a date, at that point focus on hang around, have fun and hook up. If the date goes well, the situation returns to be a standard courtship. If the dumped says no, then tell him/her to contact you if he/she changes his/her mind and at that point walk away and never look back.

- DUMPED: The dumped is instead in a weaker starting position. After having stated to the dumper that all you want is romance and if the other person is not willing to give you that, then tell him/her to contact you if he/she changes his/her mind, then you must walk away and mean it. From that point on, let the dumper do 100% of the texting/calling/pursuing (this is different from regular courtships and it only applies if you have been dumped or blown off). When the dumper engages in a direct conversation with you, don't go in nostalgic mood talk and be direct: simply tell that's great to hear him/her, you would love to see him/her and ask when he/she is free to meet up for a dinner date in your place (as the dumper has to do an extra effort due to the break up factor). If in two consecutive tries the dumper is unsure or says no, then stop asking. If the dumper reaches out again after two tries, be appreciative of the message but distant and closing conversation fast, only agreeing to a date if the dumper brings up the topic.

It's important to notice that in both dumper and dumped case, the man has to focus on hang around, have fun and hook up as the woman feel ready and that only women are allowed to bring relationships label/exclusivity talk when they feel ready. As said several times, women usually fall in love slowly and it takes around 2+ months of dating for her to bring exclusivity/relationships label talks, as long as the man does everything correctly.

If the break up was a mutual decision and the two people involved are great communicators and mature, they might choose to remain friends after a needed period of pause to re-order feelings and ideas. They might also choose to rekindle things later on, in which case in this situation the flow of attraction is the standard one.

Bottom line – life goes on and people either grow together or grow alone).

Yana is not fully lucid in this moment due to being a bit drunk and the memories of the passional nights with Igor become so strong that she feels compelled to call him and to invite him at her place later in the evening... Igor accepts the invite.

(Drunkness can influence the behaviour of a person to the point of making a person says or takes a decision that could be regretted later.)

As Igor is going to Yana, close to him a couple pass. They are having a fierce argument, in which the woman is extremely mad towards him.

"You never listen!" shouts the woman to the man, as they argue more and more fiercely. The man tries to justify logically that he was listening to her and this simply escalates the argument with her.

(Everything a woman says and does is based on her emotions in the present moment. So when a woman does an hasty generalization like *"You never listen"*, what she actually means it's that she doesn't feel listened in that exact moment.

The man should in this case open her up emotionally as previously explained in the book, until she says that she feels much better and/or thanks him for having talked. To the woman, it doesn't matter if for years the man was the ideal partner – if her man screws up then he doesn't get any credit for having being an ideal partner up to that point as most men would try to assume by using logic. in her eyes the man has to fix it the situation right now.

A woman knows that if a man truly loves and cares about her, he will show that with actions and facts.

There are 4 main factors that usually brings the situation to a break up – Gottman calls them *"the four horsemen of apocalypse"* and it's vital to recognize them as soon as possible in your relationships and take action before it's too late to turn the table:

1) <u>Criticism:</u> *verbal attacks on the partner's personality or character)*

2) <u>Contempt:</u> *attacking the partner sense of self with the intention to insult or psychologically abuse him/her*

3) <u>Defensiveness:</u> *viewing yourself as the victim to ward off a received attack and reverse the blame on the partner)*

4) <u>Stonewalling:</u> *withdrawing from a relationship as a way to avoid conflict in the efforts to convey disapproval, distance and separation.*

The best way to deal with them is respectively.

<u>Against criticism:</u> *Stand up for yourself, talk about your feelings using "I statements" and express a positive need to your partner.*

<u>Against defensiveness:</u> *Accept responsibility, even if only for part of the conflict.*

Against contempt: *Building a culture of appreciation and respect.*

Against stonewalling: *Be as emphatic as possible with your partner. Recognize that they don't feel to handle it right away, asking if there is something you can do for them to get ready. It's usually better to give a bit of space (20+ minutes) for having a more constructive talk.*

Stonewalling is the most dangerous and complicate of all the four phases to turn around, because without communication there is no authentic relationship. So once the relationship reaches the stonewalling phase and if there is no mutual effort to solve the situation then it's usually only a matter of time until the relationship fully dissolves...

That's why it's extremely important to prevent the stonewalling from emerging in the first place).

Returning to Igor, he arrives in front of Yana's house. Yana is waiting him outside to greet him and Igor kiss her on the spot. She doesn't reject the kiss and she start to kiss him back and make out with him. However Yana doesn't realize that someone else was there in that exact moment....

Diego had finished earlier the negotiations and was about to paying her a surprise visite with a bouquet of rose. As Diego sees that Yana is kissing back Igor with passion and inviting him inside, he throws away the flowers on the floor and goes away without being noticed by them. The sexual tension between Yana and Igor is extremely high and even if Yana at first feels strange about the situation, then she hooks up later with him in her place...

THE IMPORTANCE OF TRUST

The following morning Yana wakes up, noticing that she is naked in the bed together with Igor, quickly realizing what happened when she was a bit drunk the previous evening.

Igor wakes up: *"Hey! It was amazing Yana... The best passional night that we ever had..."* _ whispers Igor in her hears.

Some flashbacks of the night returned to her mind and how mindblowing the experience was. Yana is confused and doesn't know what to say in that moment, and suddendly the phone rings...

Yana's face turns into a pale white colour when she sees the message... The sender is Diego and the message recitates a *"We need to talk in person"*.

At which point, Yana completely panics...

Yana: *"Yesterday I was a bit drunk, Igor. Yeah it was the best passional night that we ever had.. Thanks for that, but... Now you need to go away."*.

Igor: *"Ok, I see. I will go away right now, anyways keep in mind that it was fully consensual... Thanks for the wonderful passional night. I wish you an amazing day..."*

Igor quickly goes away and Yana starts to think about what to do about the situation.

(Sex by itself is not enough to make a relationship work on long term. If there are problems in communication skills, the values of the two are not aligned and they don't have at least something in common to talk about – over

the course of time the couple will slowly depolarize and the relationship will eventually dissipate. Some women will look to line up a replacement as things are going sideways before breaking off and this type of women will talk about other dudes that they know in a very flirty way to their man when unsatisfied as an indirect signal of: *"Come on dude! Wake up, this is your replacement if you don't turn around the situation as I'm not happy about how things are going"*.

Bottom line, in a relationship you will not be always having sex, so you want to have similar values and some kind of common interests to talk about – in this way the conversation will never get dull.

Sexual compatibility with the partner is also important... Therefore it's a good idea to read books about improving your skills in the sexual area and experiment that with your partner. In particular, I strongly recommend you to read books about tantra and learn it. Tantra is a sector of yoga which studies how to use sex as a form of advanced meditation and as bonus it developed over thousand of years many powerful sexual techniques... With tantra you can experience sex in its full potential.)

After she calms down, she calls Diego: *"Hello honey, I saw your message. What's up?"*.

Diego: *"The negotiation was great. When I can talk with you in person? I prefer to talk about a certain matter eye to eye, as soon as possible"*.

Yana fully freaks out as she hears Diego saying that with a distant tone of voice... realizing that most likely *"the certain matter"* is about what happened yesterday but she tries to keep her cool.

Yana: *"Sure, what about we talk this evening?"*.

Diego: *"Ok, what about at my place at 18?"*.

Yana: *"Ok, see you later"*.

At the agreed place and hour Yana arrives and greets Diego. Yana tries to kiss Diego, but he rejects the kiss and looks at her in a cold way.

Yana: *"Honey, what's wrong?"*.

Diego: *" I finished earlier that long negotiation about which we talked about. So yesterday I was coming to your house to see if you were home with a bouquet of flowers to make you a surprise visit. But..."* - *Yana's face becomes completely white as Diego continues -"...Imagine my dissapointment when I saw you kissing someone else in front of your house and quickly inviting him in..."*.

Yana: *"Diego please... Honey... Don't jump immediately to conclusions. I can explain to you – it's not like it seems."*.

Diego: *"And how it is, then? I listen"*.

Yana: *"Yesterday I was a bit drunk, I wasn't lucid and you know... Igor is my ex and it just happened... This morning when I woke up, I realized that I made a mistake and quickly send him away from my house... I cannot change what happened yesterday. But I can assure that I love you with all my heart"* as she takes the initiative and kisses him on the lips... but again he doesn't kiss her back.

Diego gently pushes her away and says to her: *"Yana, you miss the point. Even if you were a bit drunk, you still made a deliberate and consensual choice yesterday... And with an ex to top that... I saw that you kissed him back with passion. Yana, I love you too... But the deal here is not about love".*

Yana starts to freak out as Diego's voice becomes colder and colder as he continues: *"The deal here is about trust. I am dissapointed by what you did and I don't feel that I can trust you at the moment. You need to show me with actions...".*

Yana*: "Please Diego... Believe me... Between us it can still work... I'm mortified about what happened... If you need some time to think about this, I totally understand it and I'll give it to you. We can talk about it later when you feel more calm..."*

Diego: *"Yana... Yes, I need to think about this by myself so I'll get back in touch when I decide what to do. Now please leave me alone... Catch you later".*

Yana understands that it is better if she lets Diego have some space and goes away.

(Always keep in mind that trust is built through a series of experiences shared with others... So when behaviour is consistent, faith in the relationship develops and when promises are broken or people are misled the bonds of trust are insted breached. Trust takes long time to develop, but it can be lost in the blink of an eye).

After that Yana calls Essenia and she quickly goes to see her. Yana explains to her everything.

Essenia: *"You know that you are like a sister to me, right Yana?".*

Yana: *"Yes, I know. Likewise"*

Essenia: *"I understand that you were a bit drunk, so you weren't lucid when you did that mistake. However you still cheated on Diego, so of course he has all the rights of questioning your commitment to him and to make the thing even more serious you cheated on him with an ex... It might have been only a moment of passion, or some subconscious feelings towards Igor might still be there. You already explained to him the whole situation so... Now you should respect his space and wait for his decision to either continue or not. Don't pressure him. He needs to think, so pressuring him right now would be counterproductive and make him feel that you don't care about his feelings due to your behaviour. Remember that whatever Diego chooses to do, I am here for you. Also you should be more careful in the future about drinking".*

Yana: *"Thanks for having talked Essenia, and yes I will respect his space. That said I am a bit nervous and scared. I mean that his tone and behaviour seemed very cold yesterday..."*

Essenia: *"Let's just see what happens.."*

Yana: *"...Yes, let's see... Hopefully he will agree to give me the chance to continue being with him".*

(Either you are committed in an exclusive relationship or you aren't. If you are in an exclusive relationship then keep in mind that cheating is a big deal as the base of any authentic relationship is respect and without trust there is no reason to continue. Bottom line - the final call about what to do upon the cheating, it's up to the couple as " it takes two to tango").

THE EPILOGUE

Yana looks several times for day at the phone, hoping to receive a call or a message from Diego.

A week passes but still nothing... Yana is worried about losing the relationship with Diego.

After roughly 10 days, finally Diego calls her.

Yana: *"Hello Diego!"*.

Diego: *"I thought a lot about what happened and I decided what to do. I prefer to talk about this in person. What about we do tomorrow evening at my place?"*.

Yana has a bad feeling, but she tries to keep her cool: *"Yes, sure"*.

Diego: *"Ok, what about at my places at 7 pm?"*.

Yana*: "Ok, see you tomorrow"*.

Diego*: "See you tomorrow"*.

Yana calls Essenia, at which Essenia tries to cheer her up and that she will see tomorrow in person what Diego says to her.

The following day Diego waits her outside his house at 7 pm with the keys in his hand. Yana arrives and greets him. Diego invites her in, she enters and as Diego is about to enter and to close the door....

Two criminals appear from nowhere with their face covered and attack them. Diego is able to knock down one of them and he is about to knock down the other... But suddenly a third one appears from the shadows with a gun and shoots, covering the back for the second robber. One of the shots hits Diego, who falls to the ground right after.

Yana screams *"Diegoooo noooo!!! Please police, help us!!!"* as one of the robbers keeps her down and gags her mouth and her hands to avoid further screams and that she tries to call with the phone someone. Then they start to rob Diego's house.

A cop in a nearby street hears the noise of the gun shots and her screams, so he runs as fast as possible to intervene. The robbers notice that the cop is arriving, thus they vanish before they can take much. When the cop arrives, he finds Diego on the ground bleeding and Yana shocked about what just happened and trying to scream for help, with the house in a messy status but not much was apparently stolen. The cop first goes to Diego and checks his condition – he is alive but unconscious. He needs urgent medical assistance. The cop immediately calls an ambulance with urgence, then frees Yana.

Yana: *"How is Diego? Is he fine???".*

The cop: *"He is alive but unconscious. He needs to be urgently transported to the hospital for medical assistance. I called the ambulance and they will be in a few minutes. In the meanwhile I will do whatever is possible to assure that he gets to the hospital alive. Please give me those bandages right away".*

Yana: *"Here they are. Please help Diego."*

The cop says to her *"I'm a man of my word and I'll do whatever it's possible to help him"* as he strongly swaddles the wound to reduce the bleeding.

Yana calms down a bit and explains to the cop what exactly happened so he can fill a report.

By looking at Yana, the cop doesn't seem to notice any injures at first glance but he suggest that she should also be checked at the hospital.

As he says this, the ambulance arrives and the cop makes sure that both Diego and Yana are transported to the hospital together.

Yana thanks the cop with all her heart, the cop wishes them all the best, as the ambulance quickly leaves to reach the closest hospital.

(Certainty is a masculine trait. When a man says that he will do something and follow this up by doing what he said, the woman will trust his masculinity and fully relax in her femininity thus following the leadership of the man. When a man instead acts in an uncertain and incongruous way around a woman, the woman instead will not feel safe as she will not trust his masculine core.)

Diego and Yana arrive to the hospital. Diego is immediately bringed in the department for red codes as they promise to Yana that she can check back on him after they check her.

Yana is worried about him as the doctor are checking her.

"You are fine" - says the doctor to her - *"A bit of bruises for having being gagged, but nothing serious. I advice a bit of rest. You are free to go now and to check how Diego is"*.

Yana thanks the doctor and runs towards Diego.

She sees that Diego is being bringed to an operation room.

"What's happening to him?" - Yana asks to the doctor.

"We need to operate him right now, please move and wait there until we finish the operation." - replies the doctor.

They urgently bring Diego in the operation room and Yana waits.

Yana is fully shocked about what is happening: *"This can't be happening... If I didn't cheat on him with Igor maybe we wouldn't have meet at that hour today, and this situation wouldn't have happened..."*

Yana calls Essenia and she quickly goes to see her. Yana explains to Essenia everything that just happened.

Essenia: *"This is not your fault. It is the fault of the robbers. They shooted at him, not you. Now all you can do is to hope that he makes it and be there for him".*

Yana: *"Yes, you're right. I'm just very worried about him".*

The doctor exits from the operation room.

The doctor: *"Hi Yana, we just finished the operation".*

Yana: *"How is he, doctor?".*

The doctor: *"We removed the bullet and stopped the bleeding successfully. Fortunately the bullet didn't hit any vital area, however he is still in bad condition and unconscious.*
We will move somewhere else to monitor him until he hopefully wakes up".

Yana: *"Please can I stay close to him? I love him".*

The doctor: *"Yes, there is no problem... I will get you a chair and you can stay close to him".*

Yana: *"Thank you very much doctor".*

Yana and Essenia follow the doctor, then Yana gets a chair and stays close to Diego while Essenia waits for Yana outside the room.

The hours pass, but Diego is still unconscious and Yana eventually falls asleep on Diego and Essenia also sleeps outside the room.

The follow morning Essenia wakes up and notices that Diego is still unconscious and Yana sleeping close to him.

And then suddendly... Diego starts to move, opening his eyes and noticing that Yana felt asleep close to him. As Essenia notices that, she enters the room where there is Diego.

Essenia: *"Good morning Diego! Glad to see that you woke up. Yana was very worried and she was with you the whole time here. If you wish, I can call the doctors right now so that they can check you up to see if it's all fine".*

Diego: *"Thank you very much Essenia but first, can I have a few minutes alone with Yana? I feel fine and I wish to talk with her right now".*

Essenia: *"Sure, no problem.".*

Diego tickles Yana with a hand to wake her up.

Yana: *"What... Diego you're awake!!! I was so worried!!!".*

Diego: *"I was also worried for you. Soon after one of the robbers shot me, I saw all dark and I feared that they shot you too as I fell in the ground unconscious. I appreciate very much that you were close to me the whole time and I'm glad to see that you are fine".*

Yana: *"I'm so sorry that this happened".*

Diego: *"This is not your fault, Yana. It was the robber that shot me, not you. The important thing is that we survived this and we are both fine".*

Then Diego continues: *"And by looking at your actions, I notice that you are honest in saying that you love me".*

Yana: *"Of course that I love you Diego... I love you with all my heart! So it means that you forgive me for having cheated on you? Are you willing to continue being exclusive with me?".*

Diego: *"Yana.. I love you too. I forgive you and the answer to the second question is yes but at the condition that you never get drunk again in the future and that you respect the commitment. Does that sounds good to you?".*

Yana smiles happily: *"Of course honey. I promise"* and then kisses Diego with him kissing her back with passion. Without intending to, Yana touch an area which is swaddled with bandages.

Diego: *"Auch!!! Don't touch there".*

Yana: *"I'm sorry".*

Diego: *"Don't worry honey, you didn't do that on purpose. Now let's call the doctors for the last checks.".*

Essenia smiles at seeing the scene and then Diego asks to Essenia to call the doctors.

The doctors verify that everything is fine, commenting that Diego needs to rest for a few days – then he can return home.

The doctors ask for the contact information of his closest friends and of his parents. Then Diego invites Yana and Essenia to return home and relax, saying to Yana that   he will see her soon. Later on during the day his best friends and parents come to visit him. Diego asks Emilio to help him to check how Martin is doing and to change the lock of his house by giving him all the needed details and contacts. Emilio uses this occasion to introduce his new girlfriend – Antonina. A few days later, Diego is now free from the hospital and returns home. After that, the relationship between them is stronger than ever and they know each other's parents.

Later on Yana asks to Diego: *"When are we going to live together?"*.

Diego: *"Great, it's settled. Then we are going to live together!"*.

Yana: "Yeah! Look forward to it!".

(A person can hide his/her essence up to a 90 days maximum. It's better to don't move too fast in making important decision during a frequentation. Marriage is not an essential requirement for an amazing relationship and it should be carefully considered by the partners, ideally waiting at least 1-2+ year minimum of frequentation).

Soon after, Diego and Yana complete all the needed preparatives and they go to live together.

"YOU MUST LOVE
IN SUCH A WAY THAT
THE PERSON YOU LOVE
FEELS FREE."
(Thich Nhat Hanh)

www.ingramcontent.com/pod-product-compliance
Lightning Source LLC
Chambersburg PA
CBHW070304290526
45791CB00003B/1077